FRAGMENTED VERSES

Selected Poems

TABASSUM KASHMIRI

Translated by

SANDIP TAGORE

Rightage Publications, California

First Edition: 1991
Third Edition September 2016
Book Name: FRAGMENTED VERSES (Poems)
Category: English Poems (Translated from UR)
Poet: Dr. Tabassum Kashmiri
Translated by Sandip Tagore
Cover Raja Ishaq
Poet's FB: Dr. Tabassum Kashmiri
Language: English
Publishers: Right Age Publications,
P.O Box 51455 Pacific Grove
California, 93950-9998 USA
Web: www.rightagepublications.com
Email: info@rightagepublications.com

First Platform: Book Traders, Lahore
Second Platform: CreateSpace/Amazon USA.
Distributors in Pakistan: Dastavez Matbuaat, Lahore.
No part of this book may be printed, reprinted, reproduced or utilized in any shape or form by any known means, now known or hereafter invented, including photocopying, recording or using for electronic storage or retrieval system, without permission in writing from the Author or Publisher.

Copyright © 2015 Rightage Publications
All rights reserved.
ISBN-10: 0692511687
ISBN-13: 978-0692511688

This anthology is dedicated to

Professor Hiroshi Kan Kagaya
whose love for Urdu language & Literature is
highly inspiring.

CONTENTS

1. Keep the Doors Ajar!
2. Breeze Talk
3. Unvisited Lands
4. Keep on Trekking
5. A Japanese Alley
6. Singapore
7. The Singing Damsels
8. Taxila
9. Hairat Khan Drown in Hairat
10. Fragmented Verses
11. A Loner's Solitude
12. She and I
13. Oh Traveller
14. Unending Journey
15. The Man under the Sun
16. The Breath
17. Let Me Grow a Forest of Poems
18. Famine
19. Distressed Sailor
20. A Day like This Will Do for Me

21. Take Along
22. Homeward Bound
23. Reckon I am Still Kicking
24. Every Time
25. Horseshoed Tongue
26. Mementos
27. Ode to Sea Breeze
28. Cinnamon Wine
29. Selling Dreams
30. My Beautiful Nightingale
31. Could you translate?
32. For You My Love
33. A Trip to the Unknown
34. Returning Clime
35. Await Me
36. For Osaka
37. Images
38. Wandering Dreams
39. Just Visualize
40. Hiroshima No More

FORWARD

One summer evening, 1986, Professor Sandip Tagore and his family were dinner guests at our Osaka home. Amid deeply enjoyable conversation over South Asian culture, and heritage: literary, political and culinary, I was requested to recite some of my poems. My latest was about life in A Japanese Street (included in this anthology), entitled *A Japanese Alley* and I read it aloud.

We met some months later. The first poem translated was *"Could You Translate?"* Due to our mutually heavy schedule, our sittings were sporadic. Often months flitted past without any poems touched. My home visits to Lahore and Sandip's to Calcutta repeatedly unhinged our project. Happily we finished it with the poem "Hamzad" on November 3, 1990.

This is a joint venture. We sat together. I recited each poem a few times while Sandip listened in a contemplative mood, his eyes closed. A few moments later, with a glint of creative light in his eyes, he would smile and say, "Here it goes" Now that the translation is ready, I find it is difficult to describe the experience in just so few words.

I feel deeply indebted to Professor Tagore a profound English scholar and to the love and labour he has put in this work. It will remain as a memorable venture of our friendship born in Japan.

I am also thankful to Professor. Razi Abidi and Professor Sajjad Haider Malik for their very help in editing and revision of this anthology and to Tasadduq Sohail for beautiful title (first edition) which he made in a short time.

Tabassum Kashmiri
1991
Osaka

Translator's Note

It is not easy to translate poetry, particularly the lyrical works of an excellent poet who is also a friend. The hurdles of language, mood, expression, culture and philosophy have made this work, in between enlightening conversations, snacks, luncheons, dinners, family get-togethers, long walks, the exchange of dreams, reciting-listening-translating sessions, all the more memorable.

Sandip Tagore

Keep The Doors Ajar!

Keep the doors ajar
for astral fliers
the migrant birds
scented clouds and
the pretty planets

Keep the doors ajar
for the damsels in dreams
and sleepless eyes
starving camel drivers
exhausted ballads
and camels athirst

Keep the doors ajar
for the brunt match-heads
the snuffed out humans
to orientate the alighting angels
with new alphabets the
wailing winds, sun-bitten colours and
embalming whipped fragrances

Keep the doors ajar
for feather-touching
the endeared children and
to wipe the tears dripping
naked from word-eyes and
dress their nudity in dignity

Keep the doors ajar
for the footless birds
giving shelter to history's
victimized pages for a
new dawn of peace on
earth a new sun in
the safety of firmament
a new peaceful moon above the sea
and the immortal beings of universe.

Breeze-Talk

The breeze is saying something
to clouds, trees and me,
to birds, nests and climes
there's breeze talk in the air

For ponds, water and hues
their exquisite fingers, eyes
and lips. The breeze talks
to windows, doors and awnings
boats, sails and masts

Not knowing words the breeze
is unaware of letter and
their meanings but she knows
how to whisper and talks
with clouds and waters,
me and the universe

Unvisited Lands

I am watching
unvisited lands
where the winds,
perhaps, swirled first
toward the lands
where the Sun's first seed had
sprouted and the moon had
sailed down with
it's first beam
where fragrance, jasmine,
and hues breathed first
maybe the newly slated alphabets
blossomed on the tablets
across orange expanses
of the ocean-horizon
a cuckoo song
an endless peaceful melody
I am watching
since eons
these lands
for eternity

Keep on Trekking

Keep on trekking
attuned to echoes
or on the route of dreams

Lantern in hand
a tent, glow worms
and some prayers
A buckled belt of words
muffler-coddled songs
and a garb of sunlight

Escape through autumn doors
having lifted a tome
tipsy with old wine
dreaming of a new world

Or you trek
ahead and far
in tune with echoes
or on dream-channels

A Japanese Alley

Below a wooly cloud the
neat rows of distant
wooden dwellings A
barking dog outside a door
A door sporting a bird cage
just out A wizened hag
huffing, struggling up a slope
her trembling hands hold a
purple sack of oranges The
slope with cherries and maples as
a bordered fabric, lobbing
a lukewarm sun, vaulting
quilts, mattresses, blankets and

and sheets from balconies, thin
but cute hands dusting
them off with bed beating whips
A young mother pedalling her bicycle
out of a supermarket, sacks
tottering on her cycle carrier, a
strapped sleeping boy on her back

"Furu zasshi furu shimbun? ..."
boro-gire arimasen ka?...
Old magazines, newspapers
and rags do you have any? …
A Tiny truck's taped announcements
"Saodake, saodake" Bamboo lines,
Clothes lines! Hurrying kids on
bikes, little sisters running
behind old brothers shouting
"Nii-chan, nii-chan!" A doorbell…
pressing youth chanting, "Yamaguchi
desu, Osake ikaga?"… … Yamaguchi
is here don't you need some wine?

yelling, "Mo iikai, mo ii yo,
mada daeo! … once more please;
okay now; not rady yet…
The mailman on hasty moped
announcing, "Sato-san,
kakitome desu!" … Sato-san
registered mail … The street corner's
lap crowded with blue and black
plastic waste bags. A delivery van driver
shrieking " Kondo-San O-chugen
desu!" … Summer gift for Kondo-San!
Sky renting broadcast from the
flying aluminum insect, "Sale!
Sale! Big Sale!" The supermarket's
seasonal super sale! "Come quick
for lucky grabs, lucky ones!"
And now speeds the tides of
evening. Smell of grilled fish

Wafting through louvers also
warmed Sake. Oozes from home
the piano twangs: Prokofief's Cantata
"Ishiyaki imo, iskiyaki imo!"
Stone roasted yams!
Shehnai-oboe
sound of charumera: "Noodles, hot
Noodles!" ... In a side lane a drowning old soul
in Sake, lolling along a song
"Nothing like warm Sake,
nothing like roasted fish
none better than a quiet damsel
noting milder than a mild ray
to drink hiding from the world
old memories die away in hiding
when the tears well over I
begin to voice this song."

Slowly the evening gets humid
The roof of the sky fills
with clouds, slowly, and
the alley lowers itself
into slumber's lake, slowly,
ever so slowly.

Singapore

Nights, clouds, sky
and city are all lush
green green green

Sunshine, foliage, drizzle
and the evening glow are
just green green green

All the looks, murmurings
and melodies are
believe me, green green green.

The Singing Damsels

A damsel was singing

Deep in a fisherman's bosom
or on the palms of a sailor

Riding vagrant's watch-needles
or on his eye's iris

A damsel was singing
in a nearby hamlet
or in distant river-ripples

A damsel was singing
on a starry bridge
or on the sails of night.

Taxila

Your hoary head bent below
hundred centuries of night
hundred centuries of light
a hundred shadows of trees
and a hundred scent of flowers

Within your ancient meditation
the packed power of a hundred rivers
the timeless image
within our walls
centuries old dust
and the dripping thirst
of flitting echoes

In utter exhaustion, Taxila,
here I am with you

Hairat Khan Drowns in Hairat

He squeezed an orange
and it exploded
He skinned a tomato
and it smoked
He ran to slice potatoes
and they steamed
Hairat Khan took a dip in
the waters of Hairat
and he sank and sank

He vivisected crabs feet
and joined them to his own
Removing a turtle's carapace
stuck it to his back
and scooping an owl's eyes
he fixed them on his own

Hairat Khan went to the bazar
folks stared and goggled,
and in stupor he at them.

Now, all had changed,
he saw through an owl's eyes,
moved like a crab and
meditated like a turtle.
Hairat Khan roamed and
roamed in Hairat.
He went far to farther
and indeed very far.

The bomb out of his orange
the smoke from the tomato
and the steam out of the potato
were awaiting him at home.

Yet, Hairat Khan sank
deep and deeper.
He sank extremely deep
and, in the end, drowned.

(Hairat is a people name, but it also has a lexical meaning with is "wonder")

Fragmented Verses

My scattered poems
Flutter about
dusk to dawn
I attempt soldering
the pieces and how
fatigued I am

Just putting them together
the verse refuses! to be one
fragments of the poem,
spread over the table top
where spilt coffee
has stained them,
their bodies scalded,
their soundless hisses;
my hands mop them dry
the poem stares in gratitude,
a gossamer touch of love

Again, I attempt to
put them together

these are the verse-eyes
here are the lips
its flowers near the flower pot
beyond the tea pot stands
the bluish cloud of the poem
filled with far away waters
message from damsels and
the dreams of their bodies
on the other side
dripping on the carpet with
a tantalizing scent

Asleep at the gate
a lovely transparent bird
that flew out from
Diamir-wood over the years
on the western corner hides
an invisible mount
grows and invisible tree
numerous colours of the poem
countless leaves and a
flock of blossoms
flying over the meal plank
are the tunes of the verse
also myriad of stars
and beams of light
below the plank dry
the disheveled poem's fig
and grapes, pears and peaches
at a corner of the poem cry
some rare vegetables
some uncommon fish -- I am
still putting the fragments together!

The more I search for a lost girl
who is fragmented like
a jigsaw sheet-in her
breast awake fresh juices of spring
on her lips ripple crimson leaves
hanging from her braids
a gray net of clouds
spreading on her cheeks
the sky colours of the iris
her arms exuding
a warm red flavor
cascading over the cheeks is
a soft purplish mist

The search continues
yet the poem doesn't become one
till now I haven't succeeded in
patching the poem's maiden,
the rivers and the lakes
many birds and their skies
I failed to add the
rising smoke emanating from the poem
the shining whip marks on its body
and the resounding wailing from a town
the poem demands "join me,
put me together quick" but
the truth is I am tired of putting the poem into one
maybe the verse too is tired
maybe she wants to lie down
over the disheveled vegetables under
the meal plank or the unpeeled fruits
or in the eyes of the
lovely bird that flew away from Diamir

but a poem cannot sleep
slumber evaporates from her eyes

Now, I just saw a breathless
particle of verse in which
falls, over the dwellings,
a roaring dangerous demon
another sobbing piece appears
lots of flowers, and over them
the pennants of marching boots,
other pieces with their arms up
beckon me and I am out of breath too
as I waver, a gush of wind arrives
and the poem scatters again
I hold my head between my hands
the poem gazes apologetically, and
its eyes slowly fill with tears.

A loner's Solitude

This, that, whichever
may the slumber be
of lonesome centuries

Shrouding trees with
bottomless silence is the
downpour of a
hundred nights

Like a fall-cloud
brings deluge in the woods
for an ageless time.

She and I

She set butterflies
aflutter in my vision.
I stuck rose petals
on her lips

She dripped colours
on my fingers and
I set sail on
her intoxicating chignon.

She made birds
perch on my arms and
I released the ocean
over her breasts

I and her
she and me.

Oh Traveller

Where have you lost your mount,
Oh traveller!
In the jungles?
forgotten at a serai
or outside the city walls?
In the wizard's castle
or in your own being?

How long will your search be?
Who will you ask:
Do you know my silver stallion?
… No, we don't

Repeated retort will it be?
Like the setting sun
you are fully spent
what's left there in your
satchel? A few dreams
and a few morsels of bread,
a few fruits and some praise!

View this riverside a little, where stand
still the fossilized rock of nocturne,
see beyond the city where too
reigns steeled darkness, and
view a bit beyond the night
where also stands the same night!
tell me how,
How are you to ford the darkness?
A star must land on your head
Your feet are to convulse
over a volcano; oh,
your chapels have been robbed too!

Look at the bridge
A magician stands there,
He makes broth of the bones
of a thousand years
in a pail; yes, he boils the bones
Maybe he wishes to cock you
within darkness or turning
you into a raven!

Where are you heading,
Tell me where? This
stone-dark night, where
will you go? Where have you
lost your horse, oh traveller?
your silver steed!

Unending Journey

My overland sojourn was long
I dwelt with jungle birds,
desert camel-drivers
nights spent on gazelle skin
with stormy damsels
in flowered camise
I made love with stars
winds, seas with faces
oceanwide
immersed in their beings
in the darkness of night
days in the jungles
my search for beehives
cadging wine from the tillers
and vegetables from earth
drops from clouds
heat from the sun
words from light and
love from above

I trudged along the horizon
repeated by apace with the north star
sprinted via the sun's axis
bumped along with the moon

Overland my route was long
nameless streets
nameless hutments, lanes
among nameless faces
a long sojourn indeed

Unknown beaches, islets,
boats and bands
of nameless boatman

Long was my travel on land

Longer than that of the solitary
stars, the sex play of
astral youth, the centuries and their
changing garbs
Longer than even naked fragrance

Overland the sojourn was long,
endless one indeed

Absolutely nonstop.

The Man under Sun

The man standing under the sun
hold a secret book and a
jungle in his linen sack

The Sun that popped up today
shall sow a poem-seed in the soil,
and a tree will be up when spring comes next.

He distributed equally from a bouquet of bud-light
among everyone.
"Only my hand gets lit!"
complained an old fogey,"Only
this finger is bright" shrieked a hag.
Utterly melancholic he squatted in
the shadows begging the spirit.

The man standing under the Sun
had engraved your name on a
poem-tree's bark years ago.
A song made a nest in its branch
and today he engraves again and again

your name on the poem-tree;
perhaps to make it his own abode.

The Breath

She laughs in my veins
she sparkles on my spectrums.
She demands streams of lilies
from the clouds and from
the skies an abode of peace.
Talking in the wind's tongues
chuckling in starry lingo
she sings like a winged being.

Checking the stars for time
and weather from the clouds
she begs for leafy woods from the Sun
and from the moon a lake for swans.

In the land of rains, she decks
herself as a butterfly, and
sways on the needles of sunbeams
as she lowers herself into my being.
It's she who giggles in my veins
it's she who twirls on my spectrums.

Let Me Grow a Forest of Poems

You pen your verses
let me grow them
My being is a sail boat
hands the paddles
my anchor the star
clouds my mast
the moon my lamp
the Sun my candle light
in the human dwellings
I'll surely light this candle

You pen your poems
let me grow them in
the verdant paddies
I'll move with the subterranean
scent that wafts toward the
last gate of the deepest deep

Wrenching torpid nights, I'll
stich my winter garment and
imprison the freezing period to
release it on the summer verdure.

I remember the days
when hot moon slept on the
threshold of her warm breasts
when fragrance sowed seeds
on the lips when the sky
was inching towards the face
with its seven-star caravan

Those times too I remember
when a shining star was
crucified on a wooden slat
when blunt lighting knives
slivered tongues and bodies
where pierced with flint-sparks,
when the sky was filled with
the tears of the stars and
when oceans hiccupped
uncontrollably.

I had neither a sword
nor dagger nor axe
neither gunpowder nor matchlock
neither uniform nor boots
all I could was to slip into
the currents on a raft of words
and lifting a skyload of letters I
ran amuck in the lanes and bylanes.

And I remember the
marshy sandflats, the
enchanting vineyards,
hapless camel drivers who
I accompanied for centuries
under the pole-star.

The moon is about awakened
you pen your poems
I take your leave to
return to the shepherds,
camel drivers and farmhands,
their reed-thatched hutments
where I will share their
millet and maize to dream
of haplessness and guzzle their nectar;
you put them in your verses
but let me grow my poetry
along the horizons of
the boundless earth and sky.
Yes, let me grow for them a
greenbelt of verses!

Famine

What hue is death's blood
go and ask the Africans
How looks the face of death?
Go and ask the Africans
How bitter is death's blood
Go and ask the Africans.

Ask them how tastes death
Ask them how looks death
Ask how ogle death's eyes
that mark the passage
of onslaught, annihilation
that hovers downward
eroding the layers of time.

Distressed Sailor

The sailor-man I saw
Tiny, like a burnt out
match head, lack luster
with a penniless pocket.
An unclothed physique,
a hatless head.
No flitting images on
his eyes and a bag
void of remembrance.

Standing like an aloof
bridge and sinking like
a calamity-hit barge. His
face, like a sunflower
toward the sun, perhaps
unable, even to think, he was.

Absolutely lost, or,
may be, even his being is
minus a soul.

A Day like This Will Do for Me

I want not much, say
not to rise like the moon or the Sun
to inflate like tidal waves, or to be
like thunder-ripped clouds
line my pockets with gold'n silver
terrorize folks like crazy animals
to live by sipping from the
fountain of eternity
build pyramids before I die
and to force my long booted tyranny

All I want is a day
to love people
to hail peace on earth
pray for the South's meal-filled guts
fistful of health in temples
mosques and churches
fly together with winged beings
fish in the hill streams with fishermen

all I need only a day
to gaze for moments at the setting sun
the rising moon
trudge the sands with the camel drivers
peruse some books
sip a nip of gin and for
a wink of dreamless slumber
crystal water, fresh air
a tidy room and a
simple bite

Only such a day I need
a day as this will do for me.

Take Along

Wandering? Then take along:
an image and a cluster
of yellow jasmines
Wandering? Then leave behind
the shadows of fright and
jam your agony in a vault
let the pillows soak
teardrops and you down
your ache in gulps of wine

On your sojourn? Then
take along a dove that
coos the message of peace
Hold a beam that lights the
way, an evening tune, and
a rose to adorn the winds.

A sheet on which to lay
and a love that is laid.
Starting? Then carry all this along.

Homeward Bound
(An ode to Prof. Mavila, Peru)

As I plod homeward
stars float above me,
winged beings twitter songs.
Clouds being their dialogue
and fragrance is my guide.
Rains bring me dreams.

That night the moon embraces stars
and the Sun cuddles rainbows
as swans cling to new loves
the lake unbuttons its chest
fondly welcoming the clouds.
Birds focus into itinerant dots
in flight, snowflakes dissolve in glare.
Distance, hung from the clothesline of
a southern home, a purple aroma
cascades like a waterfall.

Stars will be my camp followers
as I trudge homeward, a certain

likeness will be my companion, a bunch
of milky roses will peep over the hedge.
The orange-fingered moon will
bid farewell with a lush green-scented
kiss on my lips. Sky-blue lillies will
tinkle aloud in sudden
dream-clasping hands.
Seven boats, their seven sails,
their seven notes. An old wine
on wind's roof waving vigorous
hands, and I the journey-man
shall smilingly face the southern
skies towards my native town.

Reckon I am Still Kicking

Bird nests drip from the clouds.
The Sun lets go sky's fingers.
Lizards crawl on rose breasts
centipedes climb purple lillies,
dark explosions go off skulls,
sloes stuck in warts of decline,
on the thoroughfares rage
the shepherds of death,
holding whips they hound
their flocks; killers of rays
hang gibbets in the wind,
cracks appear on morn's vision
and the broken legged day
limps with a metal rod.
On the chest of the moon are
deep-driven javelins and
nights shriek from the gallows.

Reckon I am still kicking.

Every Time

I always skid each time
I step on slippery stairs.

Sleep in crucified and
dreams annihilated.
I fashion boats with
planks of obscurity and
paddle them with oars of nightmare.

On the slate of the moon
the smudge remains.
Wayfarers tire of slumber
at the caravansaries.

My skiff bounces ahead
and my mount is lost.
Murals are erased
adages distorted
phantoms have raided
human dwelling.

I light huge bonfires
but the ghouls still
thrive on human blood.

What a cruel night!
Even the fare awaiting boats
are lulled into exhausted sleep.

Ancient scimitars,
thirst weakened,
swoon in their sheaths.

Armors search for
hoary shields seek
dauntless fighters and
arms of combat.

Yet the night is not victimized
I stumble on slippery stairs.
Each time my boats slink away
and somewhere my mount is lost.

Horseshoed Tongue

Strange are the times.
Fragrance tumbling into walls,
air hanging from stars
making suicidal vaults.
Words drink hemlock
and slashed livers.
Dripping fingers in ink
letters pen the skies.
Tongues are stomped under
horseshoes. Sails torn,
adrift in seas.
Heaving camels
breathed their last.
Wine turn stale.
Endless slumber seduces
camel drivers.
Ponds catch fire.
Turtles burn to death.
Jasmines just stink.
Dried seasonal juices
drench the tiny bats.

Tomes wore neck-cuffs and
light put on spectacles.

Strange are the times.
Air hangs from stars.
Bats cling to words.
Precepts replete with scorpions.
Tongues still remain horseshoed.

Mementos

My cuckoo darling
here is honey
here is wine
a lot for you
remember those days
when the moon landed
on your palms and
an ocean sucking star rocked
tipsy on a single eyelash
and a russet sea began
flowing over your warm body

This me with fish and sail
below the canopy of the orange Sun
far, far, from the coast
drifting away and away
where an endless pollen raged

I had shot away further
into the cup of golden whirlpool
for you my gift

a search for a fresh planet
a new look for a new season
discovery of a new meaning
it's me that sped forth
to the furthest realms

Where the hoary soil
was being rejuvenated
where solemn winds freshened
anew from its womb

Where the strongest wines brewed
birds drunk with the sweetest honey
eras slept in the depth in the
purple liquids of lakes and
some new born moments bubbled
into a new sonata

My itinerary came full circle around
the golden earth bowl
and I remember that night
when the moon slept on your bosom
I, and the rafts had
glided away after through
unseen gray doors of climes
oh my cuckoo for you
from the rejuvenated niche
priceless gift here
my honey my wine
accept the mementos.

Ode to Sea Breeze

Hey, breeze of brine
off you go to sleep
for a while with me.
Fishermen's nets hang
static tonight
on heaven's shrubbery

Look! The horizon is decked
with sails. The shores,
with a tired surface,
are about to rest below
the brine sheet.
In the sundown sky
milky gulls are hovering
on the orange pavilion of twilight
The Sun glowing in it's
tandoor has sunk, with
the fish, to the chilly bottom.

A song spouting from
subterranean depths

is lonesomely insomniac
for a loving pulsar.
The night, floating on
its bluish raft, has hung
it's head on a carmine flower.
Oh breeze of brine
remove your negligee
tonight to share my bed.

Cinnamon Wine

The beach in dusk
fragrant lemon trees
the seasonal intoxication
in the fog laden trees
western lakes and clouds
blossoms and nights
all drunk with
Cinnamon elixir.

Selling Dreams

The woman. No chapatti,
on cheese, no meat,
no home, she and
all her assets were
her hunger and her dreams.
She went to the bazar
to sell her dreams
that she had hid under dry
leaves and quasi-tepid cotton wool.
On the way a bird queried
"Are you selling your dreams?"
"No" was her response.
The bird hovered over her.
"What is your offer bird?"
"A high flight, a home soft and warm,
and some lovely song."
"But my hunger, the last few days."
She said, "my weakened limbs, all
I need is a bite"
The bird perched on a branch.

"I too am hungry, I too have dreams.
Let's sell our dreams together."
"Where are they, bird?"
"On my wings, in my eyes
and some in the berries."
Off they went. The
evening hung over a bridge.
A pall of darkness
inched toward them
the first star gleamed
above the trees. And far away
squatted the hazy
tents of camel drivers.
Asked the star below
the warm-ceilinged sky.
"Are you selling your dreams?"
"What's your offer?"
"Aeon-old, rarest light beams
the oldest cosmic blossoms, and
the hoariest, esoteric mysteries of stars."
"But my hungered belly!"
"Hungry? Also I. Mine
is honest old, priceless
are my age-old dreams, Come,
let's be together and sell them."

Bright glowed the stars
above the bridge, The
bird took to wings in starlight
and warbled its music, and
the woman, below the bird-song
in the star-glow, inched ahead.
the three trudged toward

an unknown point, selling
their dreams, their
very own dreams.

My Beautiful Nightingale

My beautiful nightingale
hiding in the rainbow's iris
I have been dreaming for a century
supine on light's palm I remained
asleep for two centuries and
absorbed in the palm-lines lay
awake for a thousand years

I was dreaming of you with
my rainbow eyes
on light's palm we lay entwined
for two centuries and we
haven't slept yet for another thousand years

My enchanting winged being
on this palm's alit planet I
keep vigil in the poppy-shadows
of your soul
each night your eye's rising
stars and the jasmine stream's

vortex that oozes from your touch
out eternal awakenings will
suck you in me, and me in you

Could you Translate…?

We had translated great poetry
of different lands
tales and ballads.

But honestly I couldn't …
the wondrous seasons
the balmy night and
the gazes of love…

All that remain outside
the realm of translation.
Could one truly be a translator
of tantalizing damsels
their charming faces
their velvet thoughts?

Eh? Dare you
translate the opaque
budding almond tree;
a lonesome night's hard floor

being thrashed with a
mateless bird's moans?
In the cascading waters
float many a lotus
a romantic moment hangs static
on a pontoon bridge ...
the moment is untranslatable
The blooming roses within
the cloudy fingertips oozing dew and
the coagulating blue within
the last winter-blossom trembling
perched on a twig in its
cadmium yellow robe?

Could you translate plum wine
its aroma, exuberance, the
dilution of hues in the veins
and the solitary wood pigeon sitting
silence-shrouded in a vapid forest
its muted oblivion of unfathomable slumber?

One couldn't translate the
hungered of the Third World
bitter moans of the babes
the flood of tears
the wrinkled breasts of mothers
the parched lips, the dreams
blown into smithereens,
poverty, deprivation, centuries of
unfulfilment, the camp-following malaise
the empty granaries
the lampless dwellings and
the stone-cold braziers?

Could you? Eh, could you
translate all that?

For You My Love

With eventide my offering
shall be fish
The dawn will find me hunting
butterflies for your chignon
The meridian Sun will find me
aflutter in hues sowing and
growing in your psyche. The
glowing dusk in the ruby wine
is to quench your thirst
and, with the advent of nocturne
I'll softly lay my love on a
mellifluous cushion of slumber.

A Trip to Unknown

On Day's page I'll paint the Sun
while on Night's you the moon
I'll create stars on the Sun's palms
and you sail on the moon's crown
I'll paddle a canoe in light's rapids
while you grow blossoms in fragrance-garden
through jungles of sounds I'll fly far
while you swim afar in the oceans of silence
I'll sing aloft caravans of swans and
you strum on an unknown sitar
I'll swoop on hill trees like snow-wafts and
you rain colours on spring flowers

Together we'll search for the
unknown realms
untitled dreams
unnamed images and
rootless shadows
search for many a morn'n eve
galaxies and beings
let's be together all times in

the unknown, traversed
regions and pages
moving toward the unknown centuries
and manifold epochs.

Returning Clime

Came the season back
I had forgotten the
ponds without their ice face
a touch of rosy silk
on the palm of wind
a lip pecking lips of air
breathing on a whiff of sighs
the ponds without ice now
ducks float on its fresh waters
my forgotten clime is home.

Await Me

Await me.
Let's meet come springtime
on flower carpeted forest floor
the welkin dotted with birds

Await me by the pond
all's there for you
flowers, fragrance, wine, cheese
and fresh honey

let's cuddle on grass under
a pall of wondrous aromas,
alight in the slumber-woods
cross the dreamy streams
on rosy rafts of night
If you wish to linger till
spring arrives, do remain
enveloped by the timeless
elixirs, old trees, hoary lakes
and the ancient huts of autumn.

For Osaka

Through the city's veins,
over the decades
hovers the din of droning slumber.
Across the plain are stacked
layers of sleep growing in volume.
An age old lamp,
a flicker of flame
sways over the body.
Polluted lakes: the city's
lukewarm ablution.
Guzzling rice wine,
peering into mirrors
where hang the creepers
of sleepy rush,
the trapped ones moan and lament.
Exhausted, frozen crystal eyes,
mirrored visions crack.

The horrendous, stricken megalopolis
throws up her arms defeated
by the insomniac night stretched

over the static bridges
offstage: the sonar machine-fence,
rapturous, foxtrotting clones
punch and shock with mega-flares.
sexy spiders' network where
all drown in murky abyss.
Osaka's eyes reflect the dance of imps and ghouls.
The junk-land sinks to a
subterranean citadel setting over hoary echo-
shrouded
rocks to rest.

Osaka hankers after
never-achieved slumber.
Across the veil reigns the
ocean of unctuous scrubbing.
Insomniac stirrups stab
into swollen eyes.
From time to time the
spasmodic iris of this hobopolis
echoes the howlings of insouciance.

Images

The moon has iridescence
and clouds rain
the Sun its radiance
and sunshine warmth
birds their songs
and songs their soul
the boatman's music
and music its love;
I have a dream
with its other dream.

Wandering Dreams

Wayfarers both
night and dreams

Candled move the nights
dreams lean on lamps

Jasmines fly with darkness
and dreams
black roses

roaming for centuries.
Both crave repose.

Black roses on night's chest
jasmines doze on dream's wings

Night awakens dreams as
black roses the jasmines.

Both wander time and again:
candled nights, lamped dreams

Just Visualize

Remember that snow blossom
the tree, the forest
its dark nights
remember their serene quiet
the first, happy blue blossoming in
the shut-up dark
its scent and bright hues
remember a sea shore
the sand cradling sunlight
the crawling shadows
some figures and the drone,
remember, do, to paint
this visionscape on the
sandy expanse of the eyes.

Hiroshima No More

This was a day green and bright.
Hiroshima's sky glistened with
sunlight. Afloat were the grey
clouds and blossoms danced on
walls and doors. Glittered
homes and yards under
Hiroshima's own Sun

This was the day, the same
bright and green day,
when the sky sported birds,
children caught butterflies
and clouds rolled over
the wooden roofs, It's the
same day today, when the blast
was heard, crackling roofs smouldered
and down came the black rain of death
over people, birds, homes, plants.
The last sunny day of
Hiroshima. Today, the day of
black death is here again. No

flowers, birds under Hiroshima's skies.
Flying are the fission-kissed, deformed
faceless spirits. No face, restless,
screaming ghosts! Listen! People white, yellow
brown, black! Listen with care!
The ghouls of Hiroshima scream
all over the sky. No more, no more
Hiroshima No more!

www.ingramcontent.com/pod-product-compliance
Lightning Source LLC
Chambersburg PA
CBHW060216050426
42446CB00013B/3082